CAKE TOP DECORATIONS

NADENE HURST

CONSULTANT · LINDSAY JOHN BRADSHAW

MEREHURST

I dedicate this book to all who taught me,
enabling me to pass on the knowledge to others.

≈

Published in 1992 by Merehurst Limited, Ferry House,
51–57 Lacy Road, Putney, London SW15 1PR

ISBN 1-85391-257-3

Managing Editor Katie Swallow
Edited by Bridget Jones
Designed by Peter Bridgewater
Photography by Michael Michaels
Colour separation by Fotographics Ltd, UK–Hong Kong
Printed by Wing King Tong Ltd, Hong Kong

The author and publisher would like to thank the following, many of whom
offer a mail order service, for their assistance:
Cake Art Supplies, Creech St. Michael, Taunton, Somerset TA3 5BR;
Cel Cakes, Springfield House, Gate Helmsley, York, YO4 1NF;
Guy Paul, Unit B4, A1 Industrial Park, Little Socon, Eaton Socon, Cambs, PE19 3JH;
Orchard Products, 49 Langdale Road, Hove, E. Sussex, BN3 4HR;
PME (Harrow) Ltd, Sugarcraft Division, Brember Road, S. Harrow, Middx, HA2 8UN;
Squires Kitchen, 3 Waverley Lane, Farnham, Surrey, GU9 8BB.

NOTES ON USING THE RECIPES
For all recipes, quantities are given in metric, Imperial and
cup measurements. Follow one set of measures only as they
are not interchangeable. Standard 5ml teaspoons (tsp) and
15ml tablespoons (tbsp) are used. Australian readers, whose
tablespoons measure 20ml, should adjust quantities
accordingly. All spoon measures are assumed to be level
unless otherwise stated.
Eggs are a standard size 3 unless otherwise stated.

CONTENTS

INTRODUCTION

*T*ake a look at any celebration cake and, initially, your attention is often drawn towards the top decoration or ornament which is all important in signifying the message of the cake. Therefore, in this book I have included a wide variety of subjects to suit many occasions. The advanced student will recognise that, with a little imagination and adaptation, some of the ideas may have multiple applications.

Several techniques and mediums have been used throughout the book and they are often combined to create the finished decoration. I have taken advantage of certain exciting, recent designs of piping tubes (tips) for some of the work. Also, because an ornament is only one part of a cake, many of the top pieces are shown as part of the complete cake design for you to follow.

Travelling widely at home and abroad, I have found that cake decorators share a common thirst for knowledge of the subject, and a desire to improve their work, no matter how beautiful it may already be. Tremendous advances have been made in delicate cake decoration over the past few years, and through these pages I hope to lead you towards higher expectations and enjoyment when creating your cakes.

This book is intended for those who have progressed beyond learning the basic skills. I hope you will find it interesting and challenging but certainly not impossible.

ROYAL ICING

45g (1½ oz/3 tbsp) albumen powder
315ml (10 fl oz/1¼ cups) water
1.75kg (3½ lb/10½ cups)
icing (confectioners') sugar, sifted

Add the albumen powder to the water in a grease–free bowl and mix thoroughly until dissolved. Strain into a clean bowl to remove any residue. Gradually add the icing (confectioners') sugar, beating with an electric mixer, on the slowest speed, until the required consistency is reached. Allow about 4 minutes for soft peak icing, 5 minutes for full peak; this may vary according to the speed of the mixer. Makes about 2kg (4lb).

NOTE Meringue powder (egg white substitute) can be used instead of the albumen powder, and in the same proportions. Soft peak icing is used for coating and fine line piping and full peak icing is for shells, piped borders and flowers.

FLOWER PASTE

500g (1lb/3 cups) icing (confectioners') sugar
3 tsp gum tragacanth
2 tsp powdered gelatine
5 tsp water
2 tsp liquid glucose
2 tsp white vegetable fat (shortening)
1–1¼ egg whites or 6 tsp
albumen powder solution

Sift icing (confectioners') sugar and gum tragacanth together into an ovenproof mixing bowl. Place the icing sugar mixture in the oven at 150°C (300°F/Gas 2) for about 10 minutes, until warm. Alternatively, stand the bowl of sugar in a sink of very hot water until warmed.

Meanwhile, sprinkle gelatine over the water in a small bowl. Leave to soften for 10 minutes until sponged. Stand bowl over a saucepan of hot (not boiling) water and stir gelatine until dissolved. Add liquid glucose and white vegetable fat (shortening) to the gelatine mixture, then stir until dissolved.

Make a well in the icing sugar, then pour in the gelatine mixture and the egg white. Using an electric mixer on medium speed, blend all the ingredients together until white and stringy. Knead the paste together by hand: it should be firm, but pliable. The consistency can be adjusted by adding more egg white and white vegetable fat. Makes about 500g (1lb).

NOTE Albumen powder is reconstituted in the proportion of 90g (3 oz/⅓ cup) powder to 625ml (20 fl oz/2½ cups) water.

Experienced cake decorators will have much of the equipment required. Some useful items, illustrated opposite are (clockwise from top left): piping bag and tubes; posy frill; bell and ball moulds; straight edge and palette knives; bone and scallop modelling tools; greetings card cutters; letter mould; clay gun; scalloped crimper; plain round cutters; Garrett frill cutter; fluted oval cutter; plaque cutter; cross cutter; plain oval cutters on stencil paper; selection of food colourings; food colouring pens; sugar dredger; airbrush; scalpel; masking tape; side scrapers; ribbed rolling pin; plastic curve; basketweave rolling pin and cellophane.

NOTE All piping tubes (tips) used in this book are from P.M.E. Supatube or Bekenel ranges.

STOCK SYRUP

❖

315ml (10 fl oz/1¼ cups) water
317g (12oz/2¼ cups) sugar

Heat the water and sugar, stirring until the sugar has dissolved. Stop stirring and bring to the boil. Use a metal spoon to skim off any scum on the syrup. Cool. Store in a clean, covered container in the refrigerator. Makes about 625ml (20 fl oz/ 2½ cups).

PASTILLAGE

❖

500g (1lb/3 cups) icing (confectioners') sugar
½ tsp gum tragacanth
1½ tsp powdered gelatine
60ml (2 fl oz/¼ cup) water

● Sift the icing (confectioners') sugar and gum tragacanth together into an ovenproof bowl and set to warm as for flower paste, see page 6.
● Sprinkle the gelatine over the water in a small bowl. Leave to soften for 10 minutes until sponged. Stand bowl over a saucepan of hot (not boiling) water and stir gelatine until dissolved. Add the gelatine to the icing sugar, then beat using an electric mixer until white and pliable. Knead the paste together by hand. Makes about 500g (1lb).
NOTE Both flower paste and pastillage should be stored in a polythene bag placed in an airtight container and left for 24 hours before use.

HANDLING PASTILLAGE PIECES

❖

The usual practice when making pastillage pieces is to turn them over half way through the drying process to avoid curling at the edges; however, this is unnecessary when they are dried on cellophane. When rolled thinly, the pieces will be ready for use in 24 hours. If the pastillage has not been cleanly cut and the edges are rough, use a spare piece of dried pastillage to rub the edges smooth. Take great care when handling the pieces as they are delicate and break easily.

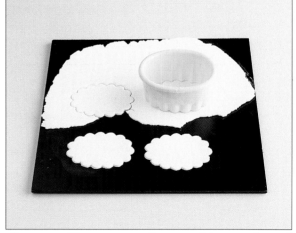

CUTTING PASTILLAGE PIECES Cover a board with cellophane. On a surface dusted with icing sugar, roll out pastillage smaller than board. Transfer to board; continue rolling to required thickness. Cut out pieces. Leave to dry in same position to avoid distorting them.

MAKING RUNOUT PIECES

*T*race chosen design onto greaseproof paper and place on a flat board. Cover with cellophane paper, fastened down at each corner with masking tape. Make sure that the cellophane paper is smaller than the board as an overhang will prevent the paper lying flat.

● Using royal icing, outline the pattern using either a no.1 or no.0 piping tube (tip). Pay particular attention to the joins, if they are uneven they will spoil the finished edge.

● The required consistency of run–icing depends on the size and shape of the pattern being used and it is achieved by carefully adding water to royal icing. As a general rule, if the pattern includes narrow sections, as in the collar on page 57, the consistency needs to be thicker, or the icing will sink in these sections. When making larger, more solid shapes, such as plaques, the icing may be thinner.

● To flood use a paper piping bag without a piping tube (tip) and cut a small hole in the end about the size of a no. 2 piping tube. This avoids air bubbles being transferred into the finished piece.

● Place runout under a source of direct heat until a visible, shiny crust has formed then transfer to a warm, dry place to complete the drying process.

● To release the pieces, slide a fine cranked palette knife between the runout and the paper. **NOTE** Cellophane paper is available in various forms: thin polypropylene film for food use is recommended, or artist's cellophane may be used. Check that the cellophane is not porous. Wax paper can be used instead.

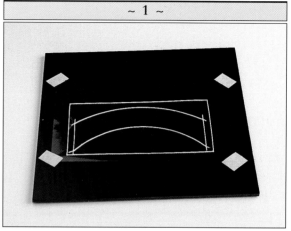

~ 1 ~

CUTOUT SECTIONS Outline the shape in royal icing, using a no. 1 piping tube (tip). Extend the lines outlining the cutouts to form a cross on each of the corners, as shown. Do not pipe the lines over each other, join them from the sides.

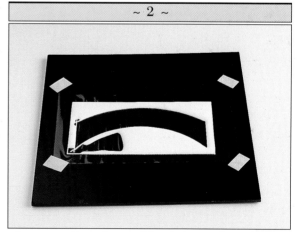

~ 2 ~

APPLYING RUN–ICING Flood the outline, leaving a small gap around the crosses on the corners. Allow run–icing to seep slowly into the corners, avoiding any overspill. After about 30 seconds, if the gap is not covered, use a fine paint brush to pull the icing into the corners.

VASES & BASKETS

*V*ases and baskets make stunning receptacles for displaying flowers, or moulded fruits and vegetables, and can be adapted for cakes of all types.

TALL VASE

❖

Many brides still prefer a vase of flowers on top of their wedding cakes. Making a vase from flower paste means that the texture and colour can be matched perfectly to the cake which is impossible when buying a plastic vase.

⬤ Trace the vase template, see page 61, onto drawing paper. Cut out the shape, form it into a cone, overlapping the edge, and secure with masking tape. Make cuts down from the top edge, as indicated by the broken lines on the template, and bend each cut section outwards slightly to widen the top of the cone.

⬤ Use the template to cut out the same shape in rolled–out flower paste. Frill the larger curved edge of the paste. Wrap the paste around the paper cone. Brush the underneath edge of paste with a little egg white and overlap the top piece of paste neatly. Press the paste together to seal the join. Leave to dry.

⬤ Take a small ball mould to make the base. Use a 4cm (1¾ in) round cutter to cut a circle of flower paste. Cut a quarter segment out of this circle, then form it on the ball mould, overlapping the paste edges and securing with egg white as before. Use a 1cm (½ in) round cutter to cut a hole in the top of the larger circle. Leave to dry.

⬤ To assemble the vase, place the pointed end of the cone through the small top hole in the base, securing it with a little softened flower paste, pressed in place from underneath. Decorative piping may be added to the vase. To arrange the flowers, roll a piece of flower paste into a cone to fit inside the vase, then insert the flowers into it before it hardens.

EXPERT ADVICE

≈

Make at least one spare vase in case of breakages (when arranging the flowers as well as when preparing the ornament) and allow all pieces to dry before assembling the vase. When the completed vase is dry, it may be filled almost to the top with soft paste when arranging the flowers. This weight adds stability to the decoration.

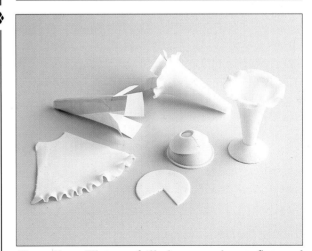

TALL VASE The cut frilled paste, shown flat and around the paper cone; spare cone also shown. Circle of paste for base with quarter segment removed; duplicate piece shown drying on ball mould. Finished assembled vase, secured with icing.

POSY BOWL

❖

● Use a Garrett frill cutter to cut out a circle of flower paste and remove a segment, about one eighth of the circumference. Use a small blossom cutter to stamp out design in each scallop. Place over ball mould (about tennis-ball size) to dry, overlapping the cut edges and sealing with egg white.

● Use templates, below, to cut out circle of paste and six petals for base. Fix pointed ends of petals onto circle using egg white. Stamp out blossom design on petals, then use template to cut out the middle, leaving a ring with petals attached. Dry on small ball mould.

● When bowl and base are dry, place one on top of the other, securing with royal icing. Arrange flowers in a ball of flower paste and secure in dried bowl with a little royal icing.

Posy Bowl Garrett frill circle, with segment removed and edge decoration cut. Duplicate shown drying on ball mould, also another shown removed from mould when dry. Base circle with petals, with centre cut out and drying over ball mould.

PIPED BASKET

❖

● Grease a large bell mould. using a no. 2 piping tube (tip), pipe a circle around the lower edge of the mould and another just over halfway up the mould. Pipe an equal number of vertical lines joining the circles. Leave to dry.

● Use a no. 19 B piping tube (tip) to pipe the basketweave over the lines and leave to dry. Warm the mould and remove the piped section. Stand the section on a piece of paper and carefully draw around inside the base: use this as a template. Using a no. 2 piping tube (tip) pipe lines radiating from the centre of the circle, then pipe basketweave over the lines as before. Carefully stand dried side section on top of base and leave to dry.

● To make handle, cut a strip of flower paste and dry it around a round cutter. Attach to the inside of basket and overpipe to match. Arrange flowers secured in ball of flower paste placed in basket.

EXPERT ADVICE

≈

For neat basketweave, keep piping tube (tip) at angle of 90° to the surface when finishing piping a section.

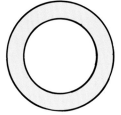

Posy bowl base

PIPED BASKET *Two stages in piping side section on greased bell mould. Removed, dry side section without base. Template and two stages in piping base, working on cellophane secured over template. Finished basket and handle.*

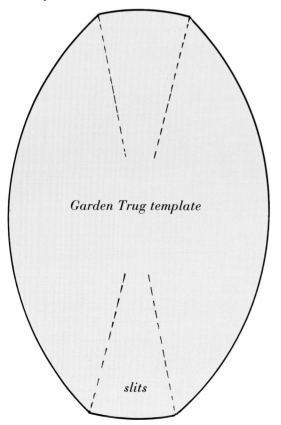

Garden Trug template

slits

GARDEN TRUG

● Use the template provided to cut out the trug in flower paste. Make four cuts in towards the middle as marked. Overlap the paste along the slits, sticking it in place with egg white, then place over a ball mould or shape to dry. Use a no. 32 R piping tube (tip) to overpipe the trug, starting with two lines of piping along its length, then piping down the sides, as shown. For the base, cut out a ring from flower paste rolled to 5mm (¼ in) thick. Squeeze the ring into an oval and place it on the base of the trug, then leave to dry. Cut a strip of paste for the handle and dry it around a round cutter; attach to inside of trug with royal icing. Pipe a band on top edge of trug, see page 11.

● Fill trug with vegetables modelled from flower paste, securing them with royal icing.

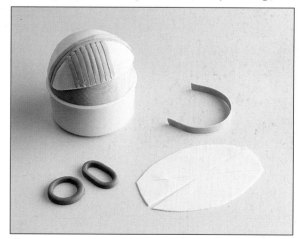

GARDEN TRUG *Paste cut following template, showing slits cut towards centre. Slits overlapped and secured, then shaped on ball mould. Direction of piping indicated. Base and handle for trug shown ready to fix in position.*

PICTURE FRAMES

*P*icture frames create a neat outline for many techniques, highlighting the focal point of your cake. Here painting, cross–stitch and ribbon have been used, but other applications could include run–icing figures, moulded flowers, and brush and tube embroidery.

● Picture frames can look equally attractive lying down, or they may be designed to stand on the board, at the side of the cake.

● Small versions are interesting as a side decoration, particularly where there is a recess in the cake side, as in the Nativity Cake on page 34.

BABY PICTURE

❖

● Cut out an 8cm (3¼ in) circle from thinly rolled pastillage and leave to dry. Use the template on page 60 to cut back support. Trace design and scribe onto pastillage plaque. Paint with food colours and dry. For the frame, trace the shape on paper and place under cellophane on a board. Use a no. 1 piping tube (tip) and royal icing to outline the shape.Fill in with run–icing and dry. Peel the frame from the paper. Pipe a fine line of royal icing on the back of the frame, then place over the pastillage picture, pressing gently in place Leave to dry.

● Attach the back support as shown for the ribbon picture, see page 17.

NOTE After attaching the back supports, place the pictures on a sheet of sponge while drying to prevent them slipping.

EXPERT ADVICE

≈

Titanium dioxide powder may be combined with liquid food colourings to make the paste consistency necessary for painting on sugar.It is usually sold in the form of dusting powder (petal dust/blossom tint).

CROSS–STITCH PICTURE

❖

● Roll out pastillage thinly and make the fabric impression by using a fine ribbed roller and rolling once in opposite directions, giving a neat tapestry–like effect. Use an oval cutter or a card template, see page 61, to cut the paste. Cut out the supports using the template provided. Leave all pieces to dry.

● The pattern grid is shown twice the size of the finished plaque. Use a no. 0 piping tube (tip) and start working from the centre of the plaque, shown by the heavier square on the grid. Count the squares from the centre to work the design and pipe neat dots of the relevant colour icing.

● To make the frame, trace the template, see page 61, onto white paper. Place on a flat board under cellophane. Use a no.1 piping tube (tip) and royal icing to outline the shape, then fill with run–icing. When dry, use a no.3 piping tube (tip) to pipe a line around the edge. Dry. Attach the frame to the picture with a line of royal icing and support on sponge until dry.

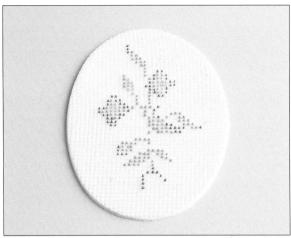

CROSS-STITCH PICTURE Pattern is piped starting from centre of design and counting squares across diagram. Pipe bulbs of icing, soft enough to form neat bulbs of colour. Use a no. 0 piping tube (tip) and separate bags for each colour.

EXPERT ADVICE

≈

A bulb of icing is a neat round which varies in size according to the piping tube (tip) used as well as to the pressure applied. To pipe neat bulbs, soften the icing slightly with water, so that they smooth out when piped.

ALTERNATIVE IDEAS

≈

● Ideas for cross–stitch pictures can be gathered from the many sewing pattern books available on the subject. Note, however, that if you intend to use these designs on cakes that are made to order for sale you must first obtain permission from the copyright owner of the design.

● Reduce chosen design and grid size, and follow the pattern in the same way as described here. Many knitting patterns also include designs drawn on the same system.

● The idea can be extended to cover the whole or part of the top surface of a cake, instead of being contained within a frame.

Cross-stitch grid

Key to colours:
B=brown   G=green
P=purple   V=violet   Y=yellow

NATIVITY RIBBON PICTURE

❖

Roll out the pastillage thinly. Use a shaped cutter or a template, see page 60, to cut out two plaques. Cut an oval centre from one plaque, the same size as the picture on the ribbon. Cut out the supports and dry all the pieces. Use a no.2 piping tube (tip) to outline the edge of one plaque. Dry.

Cut out the picture on the ribbon and sandwich it between the front and back of the frame. Attach the smaller piece for the stand slightly above the centre on the back of the picture. Dry, then attach the second piece, supporting it on sponge to dry at an angle.

NOTE A design cut from a greeting card can be substituted for the picture ribbon used here.

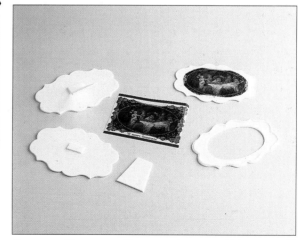

RIBBON PICTURE *Uncut picture ribbon and frame, also cut picture on frame back. Frame front ready to go on top. On the left, frame back with small stand support and main stand piece to go on. Back with stand fitted shown to rear left.*

GREETINGS CARDS

Christmas, Easter, birthday and get well greetings cards can be suitably translated into sugar, and, as well as making very attractive cake top decorations, they can also be presented alone mounted on a plaque.

CONFIRMATION CARD

❖

● Using the template, see page 62, cut out the sections in pastillage. Use a small round cutter to round off the corners on the card front. Cut out the cross in card front. Cut out rear cross section. Leave to dry.

● Cut leaf gelatine large enough to cover cross and lay on back. Pipe a line of icing near cross section to avoid gelatine. Lay the rear cross section in position, press gently and leave to dry.

● Using a no. 1 piping tube (tip) pipe around front of cross, then outline book shape, right and below. Flood with run–icing and dry. Paint on details. Attach book to front of card, add blossoms and ribbon for book mark. Trace and scribe, then pipe lettering using a no 1 piping tube (tip).

● Assemble card and secure with royal icing, supporting the pieces on foam until dry.

CONFIRMATION CARD Leaf gelatine covering cross shape, cross rear section ready for fixing. Card front shown upside down, drying. Book outline flooded with run–icing; also shown with detail added.

Back template

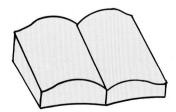

Prayer book outline

CHRISTMAS CARD

Use templates on page 63 to cut out the front and back pieces in pastillage. Dry. Use either an airbrush or petal dust to apply background colours. Trace and scribe lettering on card back, then pipe using a no.1 piping tube (tip).

Trace and scribe fern outline on card front. Use a no. 0 piping tube (tip) to pipe centre line, then pipe away from centre line sloping to finish on the outline. Overpipe centre line. Outline, then flood candle directly onto pastillage. When dry, pipe on pattern and wax.

Assemble card, securing with icing and supporting on sponge. Decorate with holly and Christmas roses at the base of the candle.

CHRISTMAS CARD Method of building up fern design; also shown piped on card. Candle outlined using no. 1 piping tube (tip) and line piped down centre before flooding, to raise icing. Cut out flame and Christmas rose from flower paste.

TWENTY FIRST CARD

Using template on page 63, cut out the card back in white pastillage. Colour a small amount of paste, roll out, then apply the texture by using a textured rolling pin. Cut out the card front. Dry all pieces.

Trace car outline on paper. Place flat on board, cover with cellophane and use a no.1 piping tube (tip) to outline shape. Flood with run-icing and leave to dry. Use an airbrush or petal dust to apply the areas of background colour as shown. Dry before using a fine paint brush to paint in the details. Leave to dry.

Cut out the number plate from pastillage and attach to front of card. Pipe or paint the 'UR 21' greeting; dry. Assemble card front and back, securing with royal icing and supporting on foam until dry.

Position the car in the cut-out section on the front and secure it with a little icing.

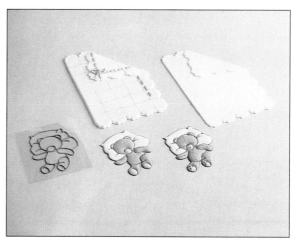

MOTOR CAR   Stages in finishing runout. Dry white runout coloured using airbrush or petal dust for background colour and slightly darker areas. Details painted using fine paint brush.

BABY CARD Details of decoration on card front. Outline for teddy runout. Note sections of colour and visible outline on runout. Detail painted using fine paint brush when dry.

BABY CARD

◆ Roll out pastillage thinly and use templates, see page 62, to cut back and front. Fold back top right corner of the front. Leave to dry.

◆ Trace the teddy bear design on white paper. Place flat on board and cover with cellophane, then outline using a no.1 piping tube (tip). Flood separate areas of design with run–icing in colours as shown, leaving outline showing. Leave to dry, then paint in the details using a fine paint brush. Dust card front with petal dust and paint in quilting lines very lightly using food colouring and a fine paint brush as shown. Using a no. 31 R piping tube (tip), pipe the ribbon and bow. Pipe lettering using a no. 1 piping tube (tip). Attach the teddy bear runout to card back and leave to dry.

◆ Assemble the card, securing with icing, and support on sponge until dry.

PLINTHS

Plinths make useful and attractive bases for many ornaments and flower arrangements. The plinths illustrated here are made from run-icing but they can also be cut from pastillage or flower paste.

The simplest form of plinth is built up by using discs of decreasing size, laid on top of each other. For more advanced work, the disc may be separated in some way by piping. To help in visualizing the finished piece of work, cut out the sections in thin card, and assemble them as for the finished plinths.

PLINTHS WITH PIPED LOOPS

❖

Trace templates, opposite, place on flat board and cover with cellophane. Outline the two circles using a no. 0 piping tube (tip) and flood with run–icing. Dry. Peel from paper. Pipe the first set of loops as shown and leave to dry. Turn the disc over, then pipe the second set, using the first ones as a guide to position. Pipe a neat bulbs of icing over each join. In the centre of the larger disc scribe, then pipe a small circle about 1cm ($1/_2$ in) in diameter. Using a no. 1 piping tube (tip) keep overpiping this until it is slightly higher than the depth of the loops. Dry. Finish the edges of the circles as shown and position the smaller plinth on the central piped ring of icing.

LACY PLINTH

❖

Use templates, see page 64, to make plaques as before. Dry. Pipe the lace pieces onto cellophane paper, piping the straight lines first,

then the curves and lastly adding the bulbs of icing. Leave to dry. Peel all sections from the paper. Use a no. 1 piping tube (tip) to pipe a line 5mm ($1/_4$ in) from the edge of the lower plaque. Apply lace, supporting until dry. Pipe bulbs of icing between lace to join pieces and pipe a line of icing along the top of the lace to secure upper plaque.

EXPERT ADVICE

≈

● To achieve a very delicate effect, outline runout pieces and pipe the lace decoration with a no.0 piping tube (tip) instead of using a larger no.1 size.

● Spectacular effects can be achieved by building plinths up into layers, often decreasing in size, and separated by delicate piping.

● For tiered wedding cakes varying sizes can be made of the same ornament to suit the size of each cake.

Disc patterns for plinth with piped loops

PLINTH WITH PIPED LOOPS *Use a piping template on small disc, suspended on foam with edge well clear. Pipe dropped loops using a no. 0 piping tube (tip). Dry. Reverse to pipe second row of loops, using existing loops as guide.*

LACY PLINTH *Lace sections are attached on piped line, 5mm (¹/₄ in) from plaque edge. Line up the points of the lace with the plaque. Bulbs of icing between lace pieces link them, and a line along the top secures upper plaque.*

RABBIT & EGG

A charming ornament which is equally as suitable for an oval or egg-shaped Easter cake as for a child's cake. The shape of the base plaque may be changed to suit your design.

MAKING THE RABBIT

❖

Cut out an oval, fluted plaque from thinly rolled green pastillage and leave to dry. To make the grass, push a small piece of green marzipan (almond paste) through a fine sieve. Place on plaque. Shade the plaque and grass green and brown with dusting powder (petal dust/blossom tint) or by airbrushing. You will need 60g (2 oz) marzipan to make the rabbit. Reserve a very small piece of marzipan and colour it pink. Colour the remainder brown.

Form a tiny ball of the pink marzipan into a cone for the nose. Follow step–by–step instructions for shaping rabbit's head and body, see page 27. Insert the nose into a hole just above the mouth. Divide the rest of the pink marzipan into two small, narrow cones. Flatten and lay these on the front of the ears, then indent an impression in the ears by using the back of a bone tool.

Use 22g ($^3/_4$ oz) marzipan (almond paste) to make the body, following the instructions and illustration, see page 27. Make the slits in the front of the body with the back of a knife to achieve a wider cut with a softer edge. For arms and feet, cut 22g ($^3/_4$ oz) marzipan in four. Make the arms slightly larger than the feet. Form each piece into a cone and mark the paw at the wide end of each, again using the

back of a knife. The arm holes can be made with the end of a paint brush; the feet are placed under the body.

Shape the tail from a small cone of white marzipan (almond paste) and cover the end with marzipan which has been pressed through a fine sieve. Make a hole at the back of the body and insert the tail.

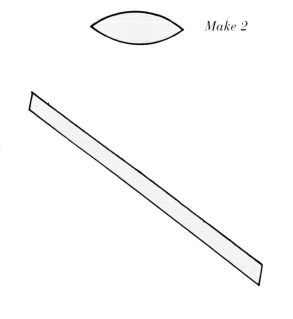

Make 2

Templates for bow on rabbit

MAKING THE EGGS

❖

● Make the large egg in two halves following the step–by–step instructions opposite.
● Decorate the egg as shown, with pink flower paste and blossom. Leave to dry.
● Using extra marzipan (almond paste), roll some small balls of coloured paste into eggs. Fill the bottom of the large egg with coloured eggs. Assemble the rabbit, then place one egg between the paws. Arrange the rabbit and egg on the plaque, using a few bulbs of icing to keep them in place.
● Make the bows using the templates, and instructions for the Sugar Posy Cake, see page 28. Attach the bows to the top of the egg and the rabbit's neck.

Templates for bow on egg

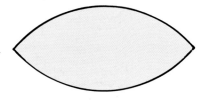

Make 2

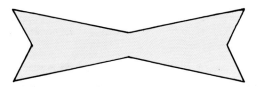

EXPERT ADVICE

≈

● To avoid having cracks in the surface of a marzipan (almond paste) model, always start by first rolling the paste into a smooth ball shape. Knead in sufficient icing (confectioners') sugar to make the marzipan pliable, but not sticky, before use. It is important to avoid having any icing sugar on the surface.
● Wipe your hands frequently with a slightly damp cloth to stop the marzipan sticking as you model the paste.
● Small features on a model, such as tail, nose, eyes and ears, should be inserted in an indent or small hole to prevent the pieces falling off when the model dries.
● Confectioners' varnish may be used to give marzipan models an attractive shiny glaze.
● Glazing marzipan models with confect-ioners' varnish extends their shelf life.
● Many food colourings fade. To minimize fading, when storing marzipan models, place them in boxes away from direct sunlight.

~ 1 ~

RABBIT'S HEAD *Form 15g (¹/₂ oz) marzipan (almond paste) into a cone. Cut down narrow end, then mould paste into ears. Twist ears forward, rounded sides to front. Flatten pink paste cones into ears. Squeeze sides of head, indent eyes and mouth. Attach nose.*

~ 2 ~

THE BODY *Form 22g (³/₄ oz) marzipan (almond paste) into a short cone; flatten top. Using blunt knife edge, cut slits in front as shown. Make feet and arms. Place feet under body and arms in holes. Make white tail cone, adding sieved marzipan, and insert in hole in body.*

~ 3 ~

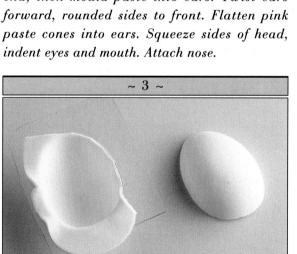

MAKING LARGE EGG *Cut two ovals of thinly rolled flower paste, dust with cornflour (cornstarch) and press dusted side down into egg moulds. Trim excess paste and leave to dry. Unmould.*

~ 4 ~

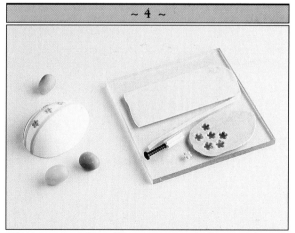

DECORATING EGG *Decorate egg halves with thin strips of coloured flower paste and blossom. Secure with egg white or stock syrup. Mould small coloured eggs. Dry. Assemble when dry, adding large bow to top.*

SUGAR POSY CAKE

18cm (7 in) round cake
apricot glaze
1.25kg (2½ lb) marzipan (almond paste)
1.25kg (2½ lb) sugarpaste
selection of food colourings
clear alcohol (gin, vodka or kirsch)
small amount of Royal Icing, see page 6
6 small bows, right
66 blossoms for cake and posy
egg white or Stock Syrup, see page 8
small amount of Flower Paste, see page 6

EQUIPMENT

28cm (11 in) round cake board
small scalloped crimper
no. 0 and 2 piping tubes (tips)
Garrett frill cutter • small posy frill
4cm (1¾ in) round cutter
small ball mould • ribbon to trim board

Brush cake with apricot glaze and cover with marzipan (almond paste). Reserve a little sugarpaste, then colour the rest pink. Brush cake with alcohol and coat with sugarpaste. Cover board separately. Cut out circle of paste from centre of board, under cake. Crimp around the board edge and base of cake. Leave to dry.

When dry, attach the cake to the board with royal icing. Cut a template to fit around the side of the cake, fold into six sections and cut out the scallops. Place around cake, then follow template to pipe the side design using a no. 0 piping tube (tip) and green icing. Attach the bows and 36 blossoms to the cake as shown.

To make the posy, mix flower paste with the reserved sugarpaste, using half the weight of flower paste to sugarpaste (1:2). Place the posy on the cake. Finish the board edge with ribbon.

~ 1 ~

Roll out paste thinly, cut out circle with Garrett frill cutter. Frill edge and use a no. 2 piping tube (tip) end to cut holes. Cut small circle from centre. Press into a posy frill to shape. Cut 4cm (1¾ in) circle and press over ball mould to dry.

~ 2 ~

Form a cone of paste. Invert and flatten wide end as shown. Attach to back of frill; support until dry. Secure ball shape inside the frill with icing. Attach flowers. Cut two ovals and one strip for bow. Assemble as shown using egg white.

COTTAGE CAKE

*T*he charming cottage decoration is also suitable for a retirement cake.

20 x 15cm (8 x 6 in) oval cake
apricot glaze
1kg (2 lb) marzipan (almond paste)
1kg (2 lb) sugarpaste
selection of food colourings
clear alcohol (gin, vodka or kirsch)
Stock Syrup, see page 8
small amount of Royal Icing, see page 6
small amount of pastillage

EQUIPMENT

28 x 23cm (11 x 9 in) oval cake board
basketweave rolling pin
clay gun
black, brown and red food colouring pens
ribbon to trim board

● Brush the cake with apricot glaze. Reserve a small amount of marzipan (almond paste) for the cottage roof, then use the remainder to cover the cake. Reserve a small piece of sugarpaste; colour remainder pale green. Brush cake with alcohol and cover with pale green sugarpaste. Cover the board separately. Remove a circle of paste, the same size as the cake, from the centre of the board. When dry place cake on the board.

● Follow step–by–step instructions to make the path, see page 33. Arrange the path on the cake and assemble the gate to cover the end of the path. Secure all pieces with stock syrup.

● Use the remaining marbled sugarpaste from the path to roll stones of varying sizes, then place them around the base of the cake, securing with royal icing.

● Cut out the cottage templates in thin card, see page 32. Roll out pastillage thinly, then cut out wall and roof sections and leave to dry. Trace the doors, windows and wall markings onto the pastillage and draw them using food colouring pens. Assemble the cottage.

● Mark the position for the cottage on the cake, then use an airbrush or dusting powder (petal dust/blossom tint) to tint a small area green and brown around the mark. Attach cottage with icing and place a few stones around it. Trace the lettering onto the cake and use a no. 1 piping tube (tip) to pipe it. Finish the board edge with velvet ribbon.

EXPERT ADVICE

≈

● The section of sugarpaste is removed from the board under the cake otherwise the base of the cake becomes sticky.

● When decorating the cottage, to avoid difficulty pressing the marzipan (almond paste) through the clay gun, soften it first by kneading in water.

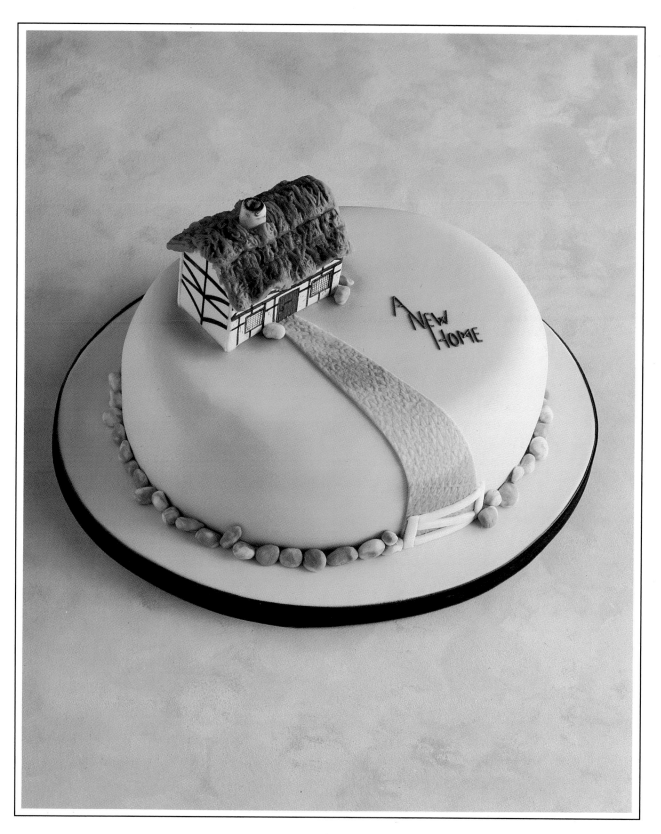

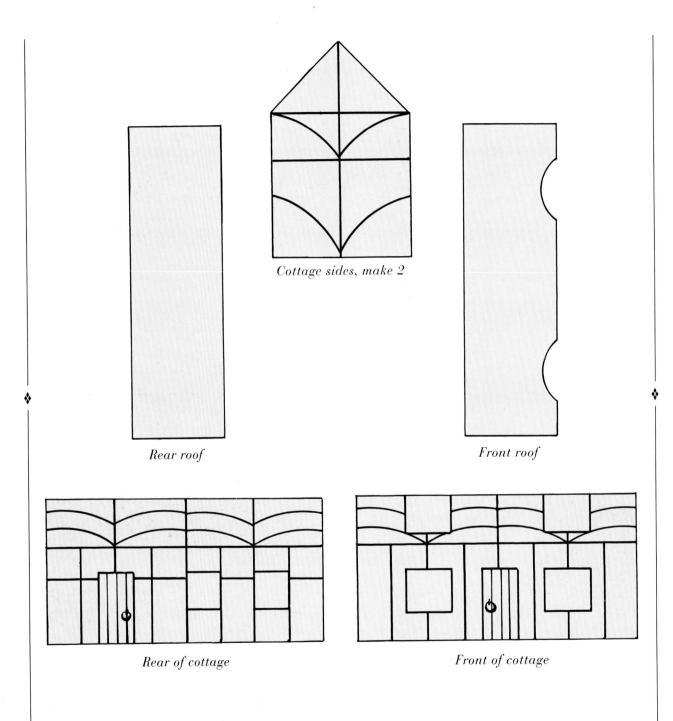

Cottage sides, make 2

Rear roof

Front roof

Rear of cottage

Front of cottage

~ 1 ~

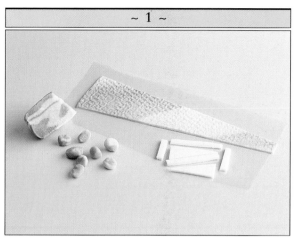

GATE AND PATH *Partly mix cream and brown colouring into most of the reserved sugarpaste. Roll out thinly, texture with basketweave rolling pin. Cut out path following template, see page 65. Use remaining white paste to cut out the gate.*

~ 2 ~

Colour reserved marzipan (almond paste) for thatch. Press through clay gun and cut into lengths to cover roof sections. Use the back of a knife to mark as shown. Lift paste at the bottom edge where the indents are cut in the pastillage.

~ 3 ~

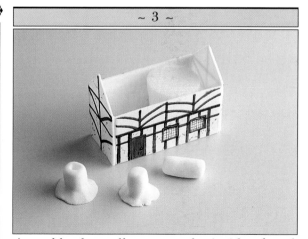

Assemble the walls: secure the inside of each join with royal icing and support in position with pieces of sponge until dry. Model a chimney from a small sausage of sugarpaste as shown.

~ 4 ~

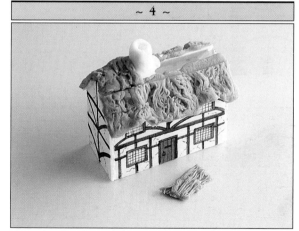

Fix the back and front sections of the roof with icing; dry. Cut short lengths of marzipan (almond paste) from clay gun and lay them across the top of the roof to complete the thatch. Enclose the edges of the chimney at the same time.

NATIVITY CAKE

*T*he unusual shape and technique used here makes this attractive Christmas cake just a bit different.

23 x 16cm (9 x 6½ in) oblong cake
apricot glaze
1kg (2 lb) marzipan (almond paste)
selection of food colourings
1 kg (2 lb) sugarpaste
clear alcohol (gin, vodka or kirsch)
500g (1 lb) Royal Icing, see page 6
EQUIPMENT
30 x 23cm (12 x 9 in) oblong cake board
small scalloped crimper
no. 0, 1, 1.5, 2 and 3 piping tubes (tips)

● Cut a template to the shape of the cake, see page 67. Place the template on top of the cake and cut out the front side section. Brush cake with apricot glaze and cover with marzipan (almond paste).

● Colour the sugarpaste to a sand colour by mixing yellow, orange and brown food colourings. Brush the cake with alcohol and cover with sugarpaste. Place on a spare board and crimp around the bottom edge using a small scalloped crimper. Cover the board separately, cutting out a central section in position for the cake. Leave both cake and board to dry. Secure cake on the board with royal icing.

● Trace the background picture to go behind the shepherds on the side of the cake. Scribe on cake and paint with food colourings. Trace and scribe lettering, right, on top of the cake. Pipe lettering using a no 1.5 piping tube (tip).

● Trace stable pieces, see page 66, and place flat on board, covered with cellophane. Use a no. 1 piping tube (tip) to outline shapes, then flood with run–icing and dry. Remove from cellophane and assemble as shown on page 37. Follow the step–by–step instructions, see page 37, to make the figures.

● Place the stable on the cake and secure with icing. Support the figures using straw–coloured icing roughened with a paint brush. Attach a small cone of sugarpaste to the side of recess in the cake. Place the shepherds in front of this, securing them to the cone with icing.

● Use a no. 1.5 piping tube (tip) to pipe a dropped–loop border above the crimping around the base of the cake. Trim board edge with ribbon.

(continued on page 37)

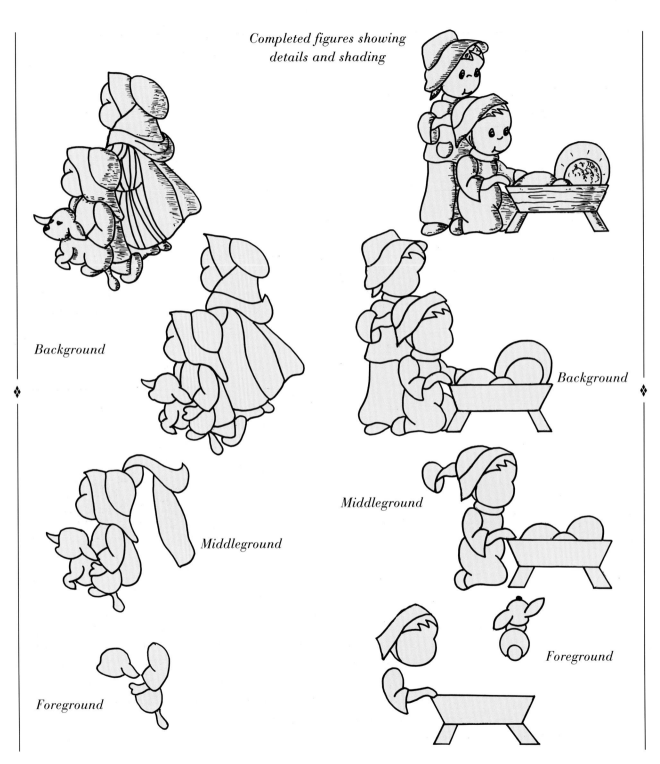

Completed figures showing
details and shading

Background

Middleground

Foreground

Background

Middleground

Foreground

~ 1 ~

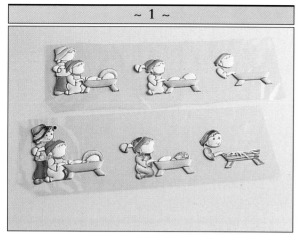

Trace figures, place flat under cellophane and use a no.0 piping tube (tip) to outline in brown. Flood sections in relevant colours, keeping the run–icing flat. Dry. Use food colourings to paint in details as shown. Outline and flood all stable pieces in same way.

~ 2 ~

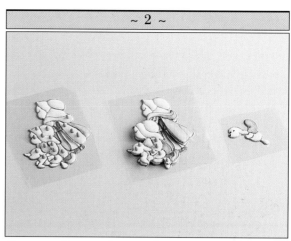

Remove figures from cellophane. Assemble by using a no. 2 piping tube (tip) to pipe bulbs of icing between the layers. Do not press down or the 3–D effect is lost. The layers form background, middleground and foreground and pieces should be assembled in this order.

~ 3 ~

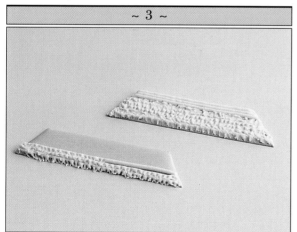

Using a no.3 piping tube (tip) and straw–coloured icing, pipe a line across the front of roof. Use a flattened paint brush to pull out icing as shown. Continue piping and pulling icing until almost covered. Finish with three straight lines. Dry. Apply brown dusting powder (petal dust/blossom tint) or use an airbrush.

~ 4 ~

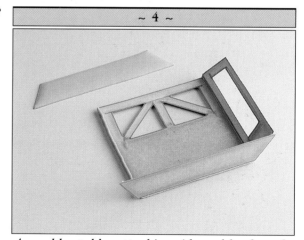

Assemble stable, attaching side and back to the base first. Secure with a line of icing; support until dry. Dry before attaching roof. Use a no. 2 piping tube (tip) to pipe a line of icing along the top edge of the side and back panels, then fix roof piece.

TEDDY BEAR CAKE

*T*his delightful cake can be easily adapted for a child of any age by changing the numbers on the brick. The child's name and 'Happy Birthday' may be piped on the top of the cake or the design may be used for a new baby simply by omitting the numbers.

20cm (8 in) square rich fruit cake
apricot glaze
1kg (2 lb) marzipan (almond paste)
selection of food colourings
1.5kg (3 lb) Royal Icing, see page 6
small amount of Pastillage, see page 8
small amount of Flower Paste, see page 6
E Q U I P M E N T
28cm (11 in) square cake board
no. 1, 2, 31R and 44 piping tubes (tips)
ribbon to trim board
mould for numbers

⬤ Brush the cake with apricot glaze. Reserve 30g (1 oz) marzipan (almond paste); cover the cake with the remainder, working on top and sides separately. Apply three coats of pink royal icing, coating the board at the same time as the final side coat.

⬤ Trace templates for the top and corner pieces on white paper, see page 40. Place flat on a board and cover with cellophane. Outline using a no.1 piping tube (tip) and flood with pink run–icing. Leave to dry.

⬤ Trace the template for the sides of the cake, see page 40, and use to scribe position for loops. Pipe using a no. 2 piping tube (tip) and pink icing. Use a no. 31 R piping tube (tip) and lilac icing to pipe ribbons and bows. Attach the corner pieces, using icing, to form a neat join

on the edge. Place top plaque in position and secure with icing.

⬤ Pipe pink shells around the top and base of the cake using a no.44 piping tube (tip). Use a no. 2 piping tube (tip) to pipe the pink linework on the top, following the edge of the cake. Use a no. 1 piping tube (tip) and lilac icing to overpipe the pink line. Follow the step–by–step instructions, see page 41, to make the brick and teddy bear. Neaten the edge of the board with ribbon.

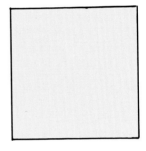

Templates for brick sides (cut 4)

Template for top and base (cut 2)

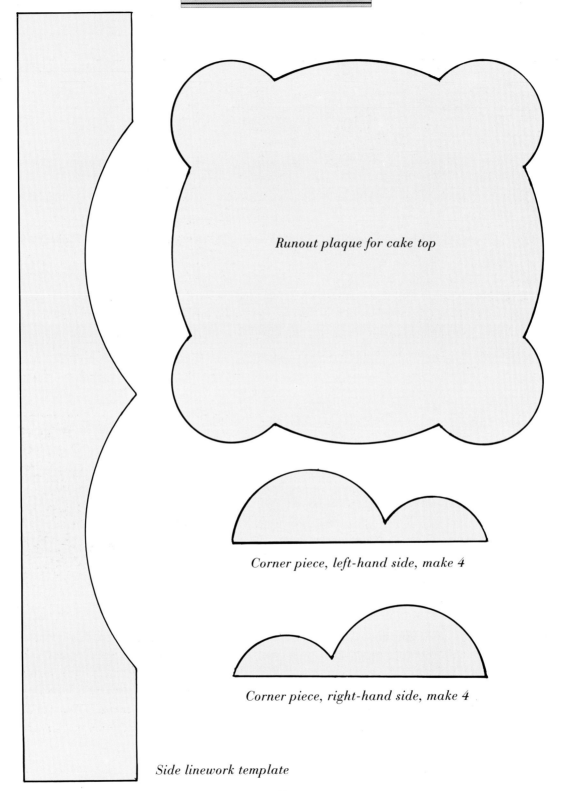

Runout plaque for cake top

Corner piece, left-hand side, make 4

Corner piece, right-hand side, make 4

Side linework template

~ 1 ~

MAKING THE BRICK *Trace the brick templates, see page 38, and cut out of thin card. Roll out pastillage thinly and cut out sections. Leave to dry. Assemble as shown, using royal icing to secure pieces on the inside.*

~ 2 ~

Press pink flower paste into number mould. Dry. Unmould and shade with dusting powder (petal dust/blossom tint) or airbrush from the base. Attach to the sides of the brick with icing. Outline the side edges of the brick using a no. 2 piping tube (tip) to neaten.

~ 3 ~

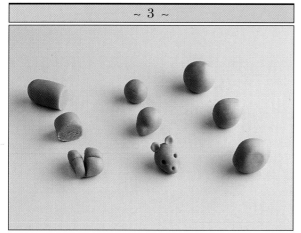

MAKING TEDDY *Divide reserved marzipan (almond paste): half for body, quarter for head and remaining quarter for arms and legs. Remove small piece of paste for ears. Make head; indent eyes and nose, and add ears. Roll cone for body and shape.*

~ 4 ~

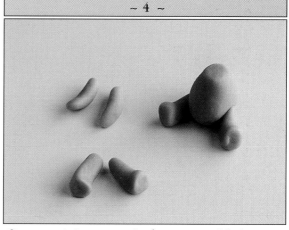

Cut remaining paste in four to mould the arms and legs. Use slightly larger pieces for legs than arms. Roll into four balls and shape as shown. Attach arms, legs and head to body with icing. Pipe in eyes and nose with icing. Leave to dry.

HEXAGONAL TIERED WEDDING CAKE

A beautiful wedding cake to please any bride. The flowers can be hand moulded or silk flowers may be used, as shown. Measurements given for the cakes and boards are from flat side to flat side.

18cm (7 in) and 25cm (10 in) hexagonal
rich fruit cakes
apricot glaze
2.5kg (5 lb) marzipan (almond paste)
cream food colouring
2.5kg (5 lb) Royal Icing, see page 6
small amount of Flower Paste
EQUIPMENT
25cm (10 in) and 36cm (14 in)
hexagonal cake boards
no. 0, 1 and 4 piping tubes (tips)
60 small flowers
5 roses
gypsophila
velvet ribbon to trim board

● Brush the cakes with apricot glaze and cover with marzipan (almond paste). The tops and sides should be covered separately to give a good, square top edge. Place cakes on boards. Apply three coats of cream-coloured royal icing to both cakes, coating the boards at the same time as the final coats.

● Fold two pieces of greaseproof paper (parchment) into quarters and trace the collar templates, see page 68. Trace the patterns for the side panels and the top ornament pieces, see page 44. Place all the patterns flat on boards under cellophane, using masking tape on the corners. Use a no. 1 piping tube (tip) to outline the pieces, then flood them with run–icing. When dry, use a no. 0 piping tube (tip) to pipe the picot edge inside the collars and on the panels where indicated. Dry. Attach the panels to the sides of the cakes with icing.

● Cut six templates out of thin card for the board design to fit each cake. Place on the boards, each card touching the base on the cake. Use a no. 2 piping tube (tip) to pipe continuous linework on the boards, following the outside of the templates. Change to a no. 1 piping tube (tip) to pipe outer line. Finish the corners of the cake, between the panels and along the bottom edge, with a plain shell border, using a no. 4 piping tube (tip).

● Release the collars from the paper but do not lift them completely. Work on one cake; raise the collar on the board to the same height as the top of the cake. Gently slide the collar, still on the paper, across onto the cake. Holding the inside edge of the collar, pull away the paper from underneath. Attach the collar with bulbs of icing piped under it and along the top edge of the cake using no. 2 piping tube (tip). Pipe the linework inside the collar. Repeat on the second cake.

● Assemble the ornament following the step–by–step instructions, see page 45. Place ornament on the top tier and pipe a three–bulb picot edge around the base, touching the plaque and the cake surface. Finish bottom edges of the cakes with small flower arrangements and cover the edges of the boards with velvet ribbon.

EXPERT ADVICE

≈

Sliding a runout collar from board across to cake avoids breakages which occur when attempting to pick it up, particularly when working with a large, full collar.

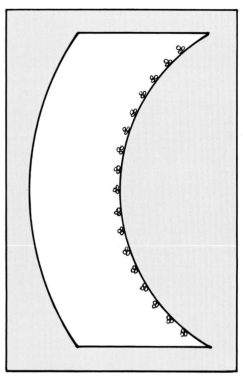

Side panel 18cm (7 in) cake

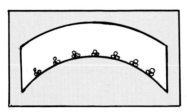

Side panels (make 6)

Top pieces (make 6)

Plaque for top ornament of Hexagonal wedding cake (make 2)

~ 1 ~

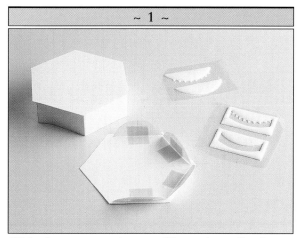

With the runout pieces still on the cellophane, use a no. 0 piping tube (tip) to pipe a three-bulb picot edge as shown. This edge is piped into each of the side panels and across the curved edge of the top panels. A paper model of the ornament is also shown.

~ 2 ~

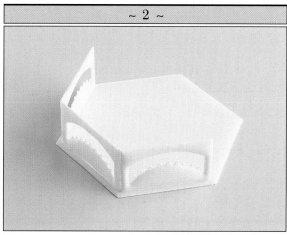

Using a no. 0 piping tube (tip), pipe a line about 2.5mm ($^1/_8$ in) from the edge and attach each panel, making sure that the corner joins are in line with the points of the base. Pipe a line up the inside of each join. Finish with small bulbs down the outside and around the base.

~ 3 ~

Fix the curved pieces to the top plaque with a piped line, then support with sponge and leave to dry at an angle. Pipe bulbs around the base to neaten.

~ 4 ~

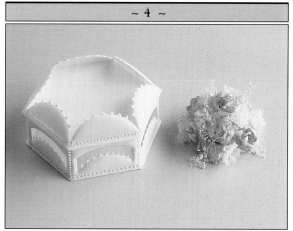

Complete by piping a line of icing along the top edge of the side panels to attach the top plaque. For the flower arrangement, mould a small cone of flower paste and push in the flower stems. Place on the top of the ornament.

HEART–SHAPED ENGAGEMENT CAKE

*T*he extremely delicate ornament on this cake presents the cake decorator with a real challenge.

20cm (8 in) heart–shaped cake
apricot glaze
1kg (2 lb) marzipan (almond paste)
selection of food colourings
1kg (2 lb) sugarpaste
clear alcohol (gin, vodka or kirsch)
Royal Icing, see page 6
EQUIPMENT
28cm (11 in) heart–shaped cake board
small single scallop cutter
small scalloped crimper
no. 0 piping tube (tip)
50cm (1/2 yd) each of pink, green
and yellow ribbon
ribbon to trim board

● Brush the cake with apricot glaze and cover with marzipan (almond paste). Colour the sugarpaste cream. Brush the cake with alcohol then cover with sugarpaste. Place on a spare board and trim away excess paste leaving 1.5cm (3/4 in) extra around the base. Cut a fluted edge in the excess paste by using a single scallop cutter.

● Trace the crimping template, see page 67, onto a piece of thin card or stencil paper. Cut out the shape, hold it against the side of the cake and crimp around the template using a small scalloped crimper. Cover the board with sugarpaste. Cut away the paste to the shape of the cake centred on the board. Leave cake and

board to dry, then transfer the cake to the board.

● Trace the templates for the top ornament, see page 48. Place flat on a board under cellophane. Follow the step–by–step instructions to complete the top piece, see page 49. A no. 0 piping tube (tip) is used for all work on this cake. Use a thick consistency of run–icing for the heart and thin it slightly for the base pieces.

● Place the ornament on the cake. Pipe around the edge of the base, forming flower shapes with bulbs of icing to match the rest of the ornament. Each flower has only three petals. Pipe matching flowers between scallops on the board. Lay the lengths of pink, green and yellow ribbon together, tie them into a bowl and attach to the cake behind the figures. Leave the ribbon to trail down the sides of the cake. Trim the board edge with ribbon.

EXPERT ADVICE

≈

When painting on a runout, the food colouring must not be too wet as excess moisture will dissolve a hole on the surface. Add titanium dioxide powder to liquid food colouring to mix a paste of the required consistency. This method also lightens the food colouring.

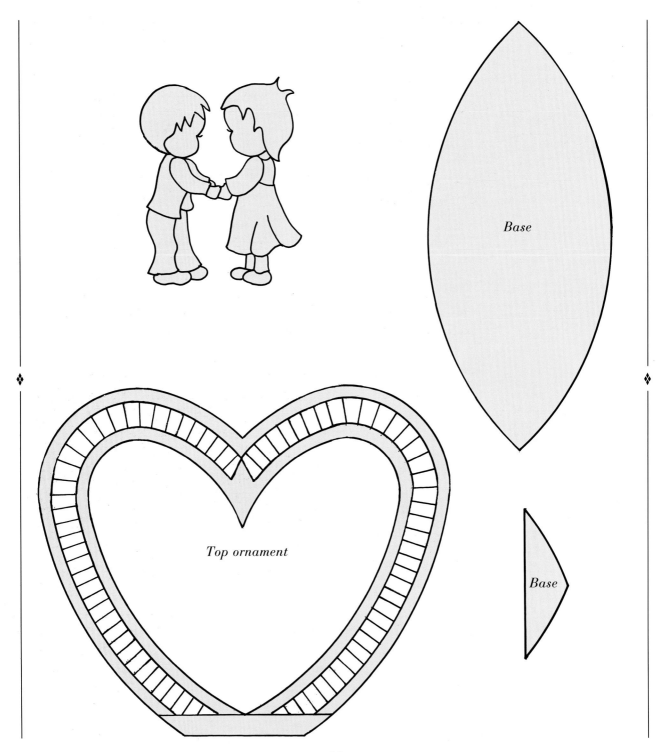

Base

Top ornament

Base

~ 1 ~

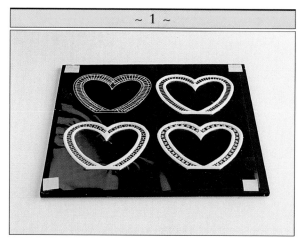

Pipe green lines across the cut-out section, starting and finishing within the runout areas. Outline heart as shown and flood rim. Dry. Pipe a central yellow bulb between each line and surround with four pink bulbs to form flower shape. These must touch both lines.

~ 2 ~

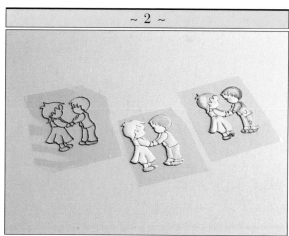

RUNOUT FIGURES Trace template, see page 48, and place flat on board under cellophane . Outline in brown. Fill each section with run-icing in appropriate colours. Keep the run-icing flat to make painting easier. Dry.

~ 3 ~

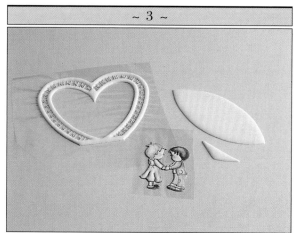

Paint the shading and details on figures using food colouring mixed to a paste with titanium dioxide powder. Make runout base pieces and dry.

~ 4 ~

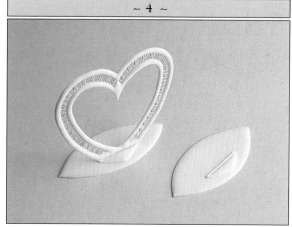

Secure small piece to base with icing and pipe along its back edge to attach the heart. Support heart until the icing is dry. Attach figures with bulbs of icing at the feet and support until dry.

DIAMOND WEDDING CAKE

*T*his beautiful, completely white cake is stylishly decorated for stunning effect.

36 x 23cm (14 x 9 in) diamond–shaped
rich fruit cake
apricot glaze
1 kg (2 lb) marzipan (almond paste)
2 kg (4 lb) Royal Icing, see page 6
silver dusting powder (petal dust/blossom tint)
E Q U I P M E N T
46 x 28cm (18 x 11 in) diamond–shaped
cake board
no. 1 and 2 piping tubes (tips)
silver paper band for board edge

● Brush the cake with apricot glaze and cover with marzipan (almond paste), working on top and sides separately to give a good, square top edge. Place cake on the board and apply three coats of royal icing. Coat the board at the same time as applying the final side coating.

● Trace the templates for the side and top ornament panels, see pages 52 and 70. Prepare two left–handed and two right–handed panels of each piece. Place flat on a board under cellophane and follow the step–by–step instructions for working the brush embroidery and runout edge, see page 53. Make separate flowers and bases for the numbers in the same way.

● Trace the template for the numbers, place under cellophane as before and outline using a no. 1 piping tube (tip). Flood with thick consistency run–icing; dry. Outline and flood base plaque in the same way, using the template, see page 52. Leave to dry. Assemble the top ornament following the step–by–step instructions.

● Brush the dry cake surface and board with silver dusting powder (petal dust/blossom tint). Place the top ornament on the cake, then use a no. 1 piping tube (tip) to pipe bulbs of icing around the edge, touching base plaque and cake to secure the ornament. Use a no. 2 piping tube (tip) to pipe a plain shell border around the base of the cake.

● Remove the side panels from cellophane. Use a no. 2 piping tube (tip) to pipe four lines on the board, 5mm ($1/4$ in) away from the cake and starting 1cm ($1/2$ in) beyond the longest points of the cake. Each line should be the same length as the bottom edge of a side panel. Attach panels to the board on the lines of icing so that the panels stand slightly away from the cake. The panels should meet at the long end points. Use a no. 1 piping tube (tip) to pipe bulbs along the bottom edge of the panels and down the end joins. Attach flowers with icing, as shown. Finish by trimming the board with silver paper band.

EXPERT ADVICE

≈

When drying runouts, place them under a source of direct heat, such as a lamp, for a while to give the surface a good shine. When they have crusted over and the shine is evident, remove the lamp and leave the runouts in a warm place to dry out.

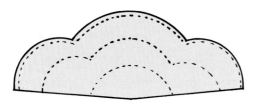

Base for numbers, make 2

2 of each required

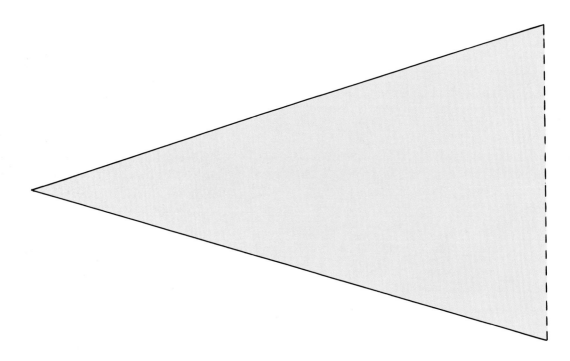

Diamond Wedding Cake: base plaque for ornament.
(Place broken line along a fold to trace complete plaque)

~ 1 ~

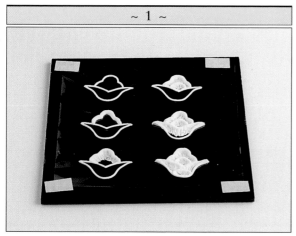

Outline using a no.1 piping tube (tip). Use a no. 2 tube along dotted line. Using a flattened paint brush, brush inside edge of line to centre of flower. Overpipe the edge of brushed section with a no. 2 tube and repeat until the area is covered.

~ 2 ~

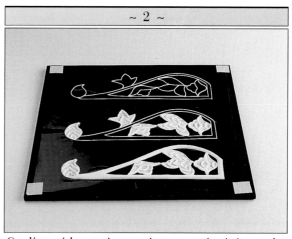

Outline side sections using a no.1 piping tube (tip). Fill flowers and leaves as in Step 1. Do not make these too thin as holes will show when pieces are removed from the cellophane. Fill in the border with thick consistency run–icing. Make top panels in the same way.

~ 3 ~

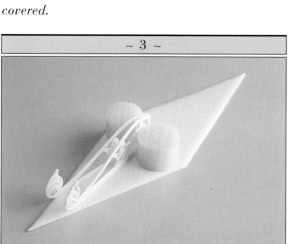

Pipe a small bulb of icing to mark the centre of the top plaque. Place two top panels on plaque, lining up from the centre to the outer edge. Secure with a line of royal icing underneath and support with foam until dry. Repeat with remaining panels.

~ 4 ~

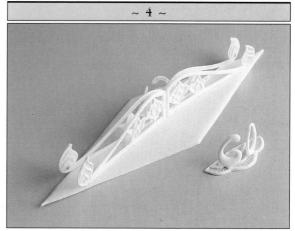

Fasten the numbers to their bases with icing and support until dry. Place one against each side of the centre panels and use a no. 1 piping tube (tip) to pipe bulbs around the edge to secure the numbers to plaque. Continue piping bulbs along the edges of the panels.

EXHIBITION CAKE

*E*xhibition and competition cakes are often executed on dummies; however, the instructions here are based on decorating a real cake.

20cm (8 in) round cake
apricot glaze
1kg (2 lb) marzipan (almond paste)
selection of food colourings
1.5kg (3 lb) Royal Icing, see page 6
EQUIPMENT
18cm (7 in) round cake card
two 15cm (6 in) round cake boards
30cm (12 in) round cake board
no. 0, 1 and 1.5 piping tubes (tips)
stencil paper
small curved formers
ribbon to trim board

● Brush the cake with apricot glaze and cover with marzipan (almond paste), covering top and sides separately. Leave for 48 hours to dry. Support the cake on the cake card all the time as you work on the coating of pale pink royal icing. Coat the top of the cake and dry.

● Stick the two 15cm (6 in) cake boards together, place in the centre of the turntable and stand the cake on top. The card under the cake supports the overhang. Coat the sides of the cake with icing to give smooth, even top and bottom edges.

● Apply sufficient coats of icing to the cake to achieve a fine finish, softening down the icing after the first coat. Carefully smooth away any rough edges between the coats. Coat the large cake board with icing as for the top of the cake.

● When the coating is complete and dried, place the cake still on its card, in the centre of the iced board. Leaving the card in place keeps the underside of the cake dry and prevents the cake from discolouring the icing on the board. Fill in the gap between the cake and board with piping consistency icing and smooth it neatly to match the sides.

● Trace the collar templates, see page 57 and place them flat on boards under cellophane. Follow the step–by–step instructions for making the collars, see page 56, working in icing of the same base colour as the cake. The bulbs of icing piped between the lines are a deeper shade of the same colour. Pipe the rosebuds following the step–by–step instructions on page 56 and leave to dry.

● Cut a strip of paper the same height and circumference as the cake. Fold it into four sections and trace the side–design template onto it, see page 58. Repeat on each quarter of paper. You may have to adjust the scallops slightly to allow for the exact thickness of icing on your cake. Cut out the pattern and place the template around the cake, securing it at the join with masking tape.

● Pipe all linework using a no. 0 piping tube (tip). Pipe one line in the base colour following the top of the template all around the cake. Remove the template. Pipe two more lines below the first one: the space between the lines should be the same as the width of the piped line. Overpipe the first and second lines, again in the base colour; then overpipe the first line again in a darker shade of icing, giving a three-line height. Attach a row of rosebuds, graduated in size, on each section, as indicated on the side template.

(continued on page 56)

(continued from page 54)

● Remove collar pieces for the board from the cellophane and place in position. Align them with the pattern of the linework on the cake sides. Use a no. 1 piping tube (tip) to pipe a plain shell border where collar meets the cake, to secure it in place. Pipe the linework around the outside of the collar edge using a no. 0 piping tube (tip) in the same sequence used on the sides on the cake. The three–line height is

● Release the top collar from the cellophane and place on top of the cake or slide it onto the cake if you are concerned about breaking it. Use a no. 1 piping tube (tip) and work from underneath the collar, pipe bulbs of icing at the top edge of the cake, under the collar. This secures the collar to the cake. Pipe the linework inside the top collar, following same sequence as before.

EXPERT ADVICE

≈

When piping linework, pay particular attention to creating neat joins. Moisten the end of the piping tube (tip) on a damp cloth slightly before piping and always try to form the join from the side of the previous line, rather than from the end. Tilting the cake helps when piping dropped loops. To pipe the vertical lines position the cake so that the line you are piping is directly in front of you.

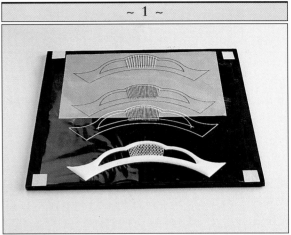

~ 1 ~

COLLAR PIECES Use a no. 0 piping tube (tip) to pipe insert lines starting and finishing within the runout area. Repeat, piping an extra line in each space. Pipe the outline over the insert lines. Flood with run–icing and dry. Pipe staggered bulbs between, and touching, lines.

~ 2 ~

ROSEBUDS Use a no. 1 piping tube (tip) to pipe a pink bulb, pulling icing to a point. Use a no. 0 piping tube (tip) to pipe green lines from the rounded end of the bulb down each side, then pipe down the centre on top. Pipe a green bulb at the top to finish. Pipe rosebuds in three sizes.

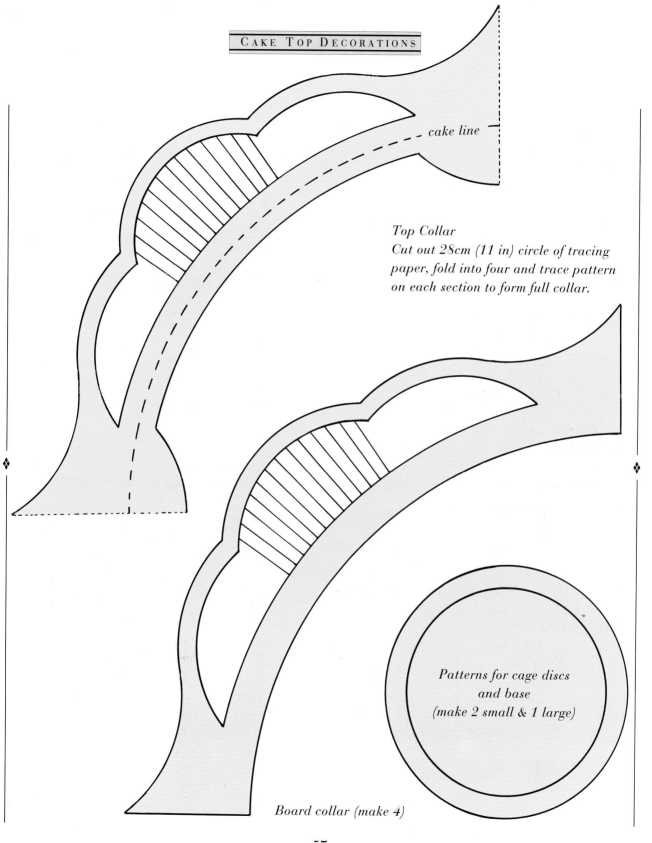

cake line

Top Collar
Cut out 28cm (11 in) circle of tracing
paper, fold into four and trace pattern
on each section to form full collar.

Patterns for cage discs
and base
(make 2 small & 1 large)

Board collar (make 4)

Piped petal, make 4

Stencilled petal, make 8

Exhibition cakes tend to be deeper to allow room for side decoration to demonstrate skills. This template is designed to fit a cake of 8.5cm (3 ½ in) finished depth, therefore it is important to start with a cake of sufficient depth.

Side linework template

EXHIBITION CAKE: MAKING THE TOP ORNAMENT

❖

Using a no.0 piping tube (tip) outline the three disc templates, see page 57, on cellophane. Flood with run–icing and dry. Remove from cellophane. Take a piece of foam, smaller than the diameter of the discs but large enough to hold the top one level, and sandwich it between the discs. The height of the foam depends on how adventurous you are: the one shown is about 2.5cm (1 in) high. Have the work at eye level when piping the vertical lines and follow the step–by–step instructions opposite.

The inside, smaller, outline petals are piped in a darker shade than the outer base–coloured shapes. Pipe four petals for the top. Make eight stencilled petals: four for the top and four for the board.

To make the stencilled petals, trace the shape on the stencil paper, then cut out the shapes with a scalpel or craft knife. Four petal shapes on one stencil works well; however separate the wet petals by cutting the cellophane before drying them on the outside of the curved former. Place the stencil over cellophane and smooth piping consistency royal icing across to fill pattern. Remove the stencil. Place the petals over a curved former to dry. When dry the cellophane gives a shiny surface.

Attach a small rosebud to the base of each stencilled petal. Arrange the petals on the ornament and complete the decoration. Place the ornament in the centre of the cake and pipe bulbs in a deeper shade around the edge, touching the surface of the cake. Attach a stencilled petal over the joins on the board collar. Trim the board with matching ribbon.

~ 1 ~

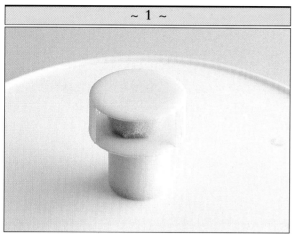

MAKING THE CAGE Line the discs up and use a no. 0 piping tube (tip) to pipe vertical lines from slightly under the top to the base edge. The gap between the lines is the same as the width of the lines. Continue piping for two–thirds of the circumference. Leave to dry.

~ 2 ~

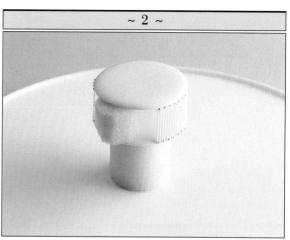

Pipe a bulb between alternate pairs of lines, top and bottom, to strengthen. Dry completely, then remove the sponge with a pair of tweezers, grasping the cage by the base. Finish piping the rest of the lines and bulbs.

~ 3 ~

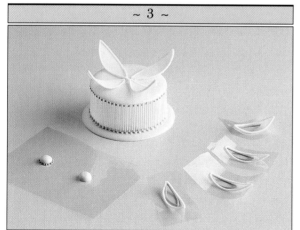

Place the cage on the base and secure with bulbs of icing around the bottom edge. Pipe small petals on cellophane paper using a no. 1 piping tube (tip) and dry them inside the curved former. Stencil larger petals on cellophane paper and dry over the curve. Pipe bulbs of icing and surrounding dots for centre; dry.

~ 4 ~

Overpipe the edges of the stencilled petals using a no. 0 piping tube (tip). Mark centre of cage with bulb of icing, and arrange petals around this. Arrange the rosebuds on petals, securing with icing and add the bulb to the centre of the flower.

TEMPLATES

Picture Frames, see pages 14 - 17

*Baby picture templates
(broken line represents pastillage
plaque).*

Supports

Ribbon picture template

Supports

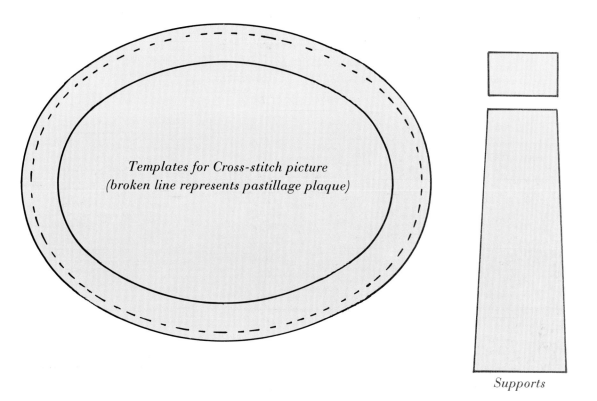

*Templates for Cross-stitch picture
(broken line represents pastillage plaque)*

Supports

Tall Vase, see page 10

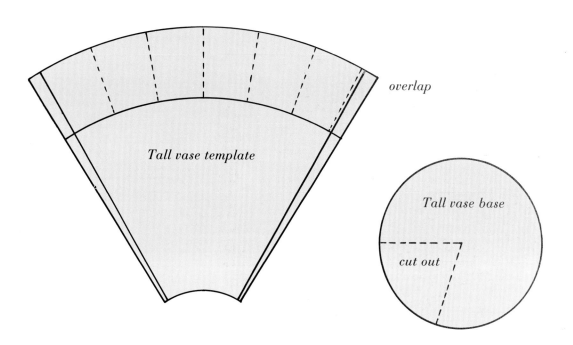

overlap

Tall vase template

Tall vase base

cut out

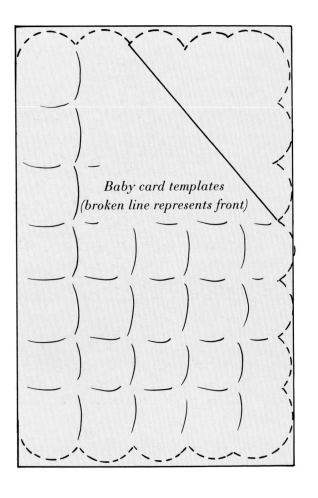

*Baby card templates
(broken line represents front)*

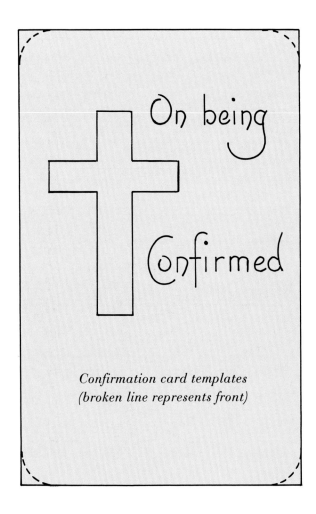

On being

Confirmed

*Confirmation card templates
(broken line represents front)*

Greetings

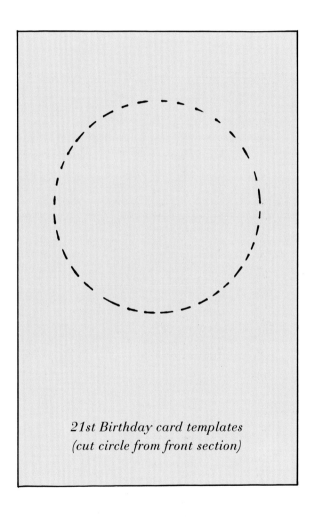

*21st Birthday card templates
(cut circle from front section)*

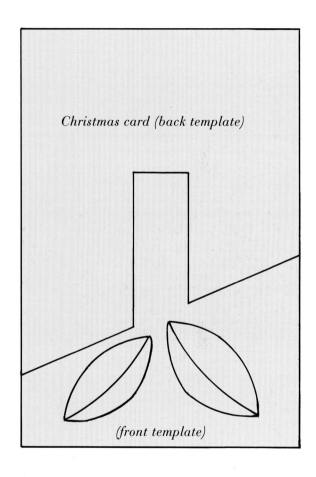

Christmas card (back template)

(front template)

Plinths, see pages 22 - 23

Lace pieces for plinth (make 4 of each)

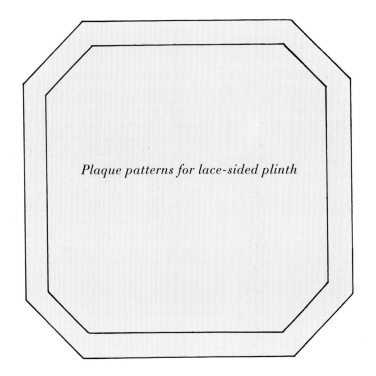

Plaque patterns for lace-sided plinth

Cottage Cake, see pages 30 - 33

A New Home

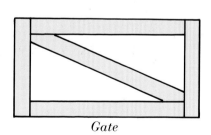

Gate

Path

Nativity Cake, see pages 34 - 37

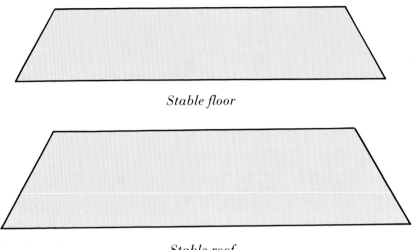

Stable floor

Stable roof

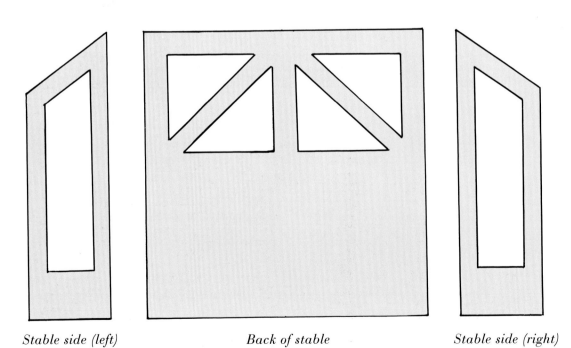

Stable side (left)   *Back of stable*   *Stable side (right)*

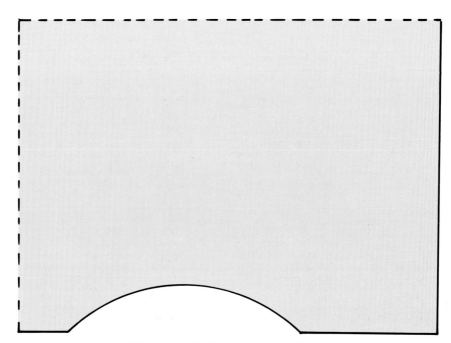

Template for Nativity cake shape
Cut a piece of greaseproof paper (parchment) 23cm x 16.5cm(9 x 6½ in) fold into four.
Place front right section over template, trace and cut out insert.

Heart-shaped Engagement Cake, see pages 46 - 49

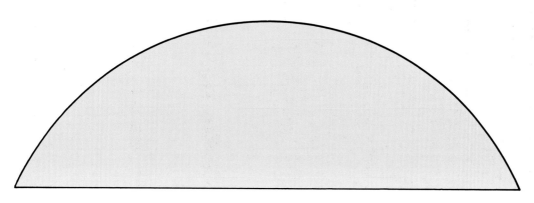

Crimping template for heart-shaped cake.

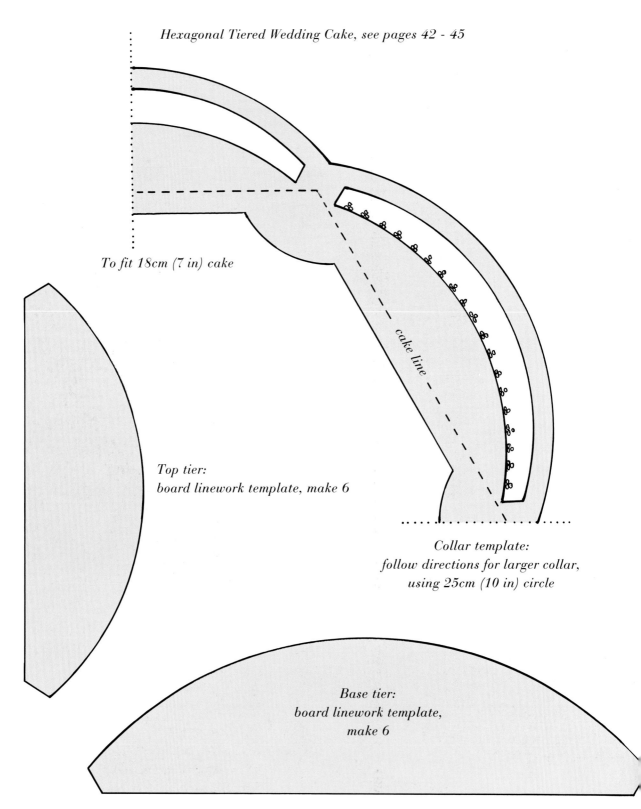

Hexagonal Tiered Wedding Cake, see pages 42 - 45

To fit 18cm (7 in) cake

cake line

Top tier:
board linework template, make 6

Collar template:
follow directions for larger collar,
using 25cm (10 in) circle

Base tier:
board linework template,
make 6

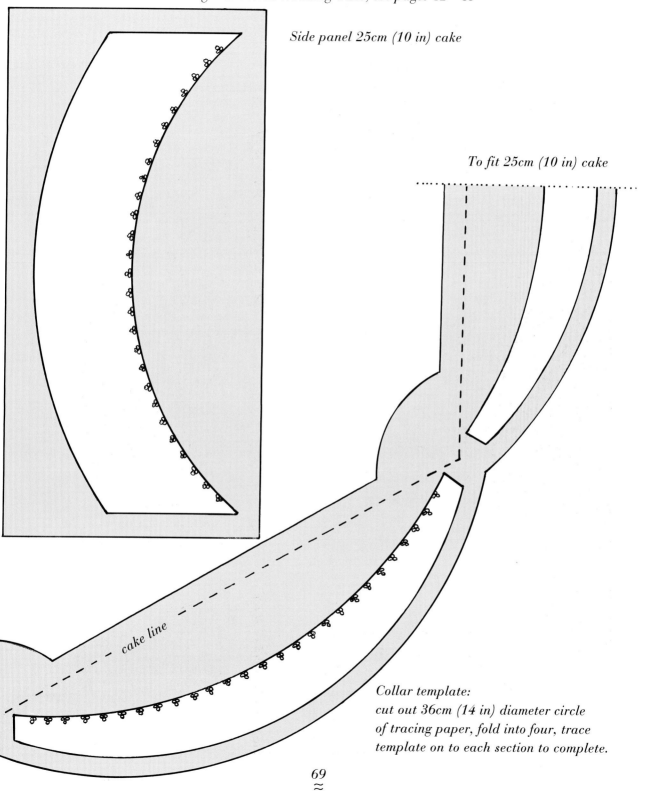

Hexagonal Tiered Wedding Cake, see pages 42 - 45

Side panel 25cm (10 in) cake

To fit 25cm (10 in) cake

cake line

Collar template:
cut out 36cm (14 in) diameter circle
of tracing paper, fold into four, trace
template on to each section to complete.

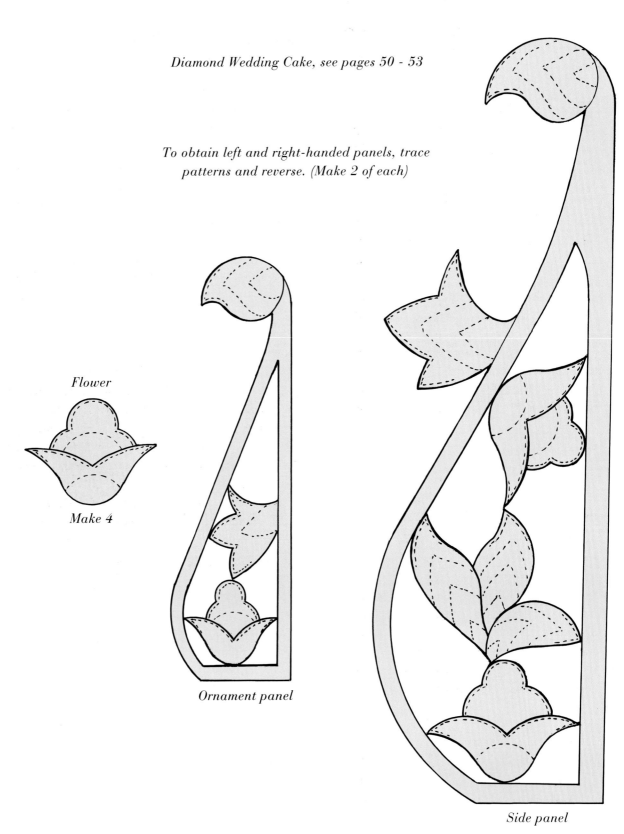

Diamond Wedding Cake, see pages 50 - 53

To obtain left and right-handed panels, trace patterns and reverse. (Make 2 of each)

Flower

Make 4

Ornament panel

Side panel

*I*f you take all these points into consideration the result will be a pleasing cake, befitting all your hard work, which will arrive at its destination in one piece.

STYLE

❖

Matching the style of a cake top decoration to the choice of the icing medium is important when planning a cake.

Sharp, crisp geometrical lines are more suited to a royal iced cake with a definite edge and outline while curves and frills often look more at home on softer, curved edges of sugarpaste coating.

As far as possible, match the shape of the ornament with the cake, or alternatively, place the ornament on a plaque the same shape as the cake.

SIZE

❖

Plan the size of the ornament so that it does not overpower the cake, but is complementary. Be careful where height is concerned as this must be in proportion to the cake.

Start by drawing a scale plan of the cake and, if necessary, cut out a paper model of the ornament to help visualise the finished result. Remember to include any greeting or inscription on the plan. Avoid overcrowding – a well coated cake does not need excessive decoration.

COLOUR

❖

Plan the colour scheme carefully: Choice of colour for the ornament should reflect the colour on the cake, and vice versa. This helps to create design harmony between the two, instead of the ornament appearing to be an added extra on the cake.

When decorations are made in the same base colour as the cake, make these at the same time, or soon after, coating, with the same batch of icing if possible.

Food colours can fade in sunlight, and varying tints may be the result if care is not taken. Always keep coloured cakes and ornaments in boxes or in a dark cupboard when not working on them to avoid discolouration.

TRANSPORTING CAKES

❖

Once secured in place on the cake, even very delicate ornaments are surprisingly resilient.

I have found the best way of transporting a cake is by placing it inside a wooden box, with a piece of foam under the cake to stop it from moving. Dampness is a very real enemy and can cause the complete collapse of delicate work. Never leave the cake, even in a box, in a damp atmosphere or a car, for longer than necessary, and certainly never overnight.

INDEX

FOR FURTHER INFORMATION

Merehurst is the leading publisher of cake decorating books and has an excellent range of titles to suit cake decorators of all levels.
Please send for a free catalogue, stating the title of this book:–

United Kingdom
Marketing Department
Merehurst Ltd.
Ferry House
51–57 Lacy Road
London SW15 1PR
Tel: 081 780 1177
Fax: 081 780 1714

U.S.A/Canada
Foxwood International Ltd.
P.O. Box 267
145 Queen Street S.
Mississauga, Ontario
L5M 2B8 Canada
Tel: (1) 416 567 4800
Fax: (1) 416 567 4681

Australia
J.B. Fairfax Ltd.
80 McLachlan Avenue
Rushcutters Bay
NSW 2011
Tel: (61) 2 361 6366
Fax: (61) 2 360 6262

Other Territories
For further information
contact:
International Sales
Department at United
Kingdom address.